Starting a Successful Blog

Share Your Passion and Turn It into a Business

Sara K. Sandhu

Contents

Introduction

You've thought of starting your own blog, but all the techy stuff intimidates you, and you have no clue where to start from. This is completely understandable.

This book is going to solve your problem and take you by the hand to start a successful blog. I've put all my knowledge and experience of blogging in this book for you.

I've been blogging for more than two years and enjoyed every step of the process. I'm sure you will too if you follow all the steps laid out in the book. I've always been an avid reader and writer. I loved studying science, especially zoology, botany, and human physiology, so I graduated with a bachelor of science degree.

Then I wanted to continue pursuing a master of science degree in genetics in a prestigious university but stopped after a month because I did not find it interesting. So I switched to studying literature and finished my master of arts degree in literature. Learning about classic authors such as Shakespeare, Milton, Wordsworth, and Coleridge and their works was fascinating to me.

When I started blogging, I found it to be a very good tool aside from social media platforms such as Facebook, Twitter, YouTube, and Instagram to educate my audience. Before blogging, I'd been working with my husband in his brick-and-mortar business in New York City for many years. I've had a variety of jobs because I wanted to explore the outside world for a change, but then I wanted to be my own boss, so I started my online business with my own blog and loved all the freedom and flexibility that came with it. Online business can sometimes be solitary and involve too much work, but I have a very strong work ethic in my daily operation that led to all the success in my business.

Blogging is an excellent way to stay connected and build relationships with your audience or customers who can serve you well in your business in the long run, either online or offline.

I promise that you'll get all my experience and knowledge that I've learned by participating in personal private coaching sessions, attending network marketing events, reading business books, taking courses, and attending live masterminds and live classes by top industry leaders for the past two to three years.

You're about to read all the seven steps to start a blog that have proven results. Each chapter provides concise, exact information to start your own blog. If you follow all the steps revealed in the book, it is highly possible that your blog can be a good source of income for you!

Bonus

Hi there!

Greetings from New York!

Great to meet you!

I'm excited for your blogging journey. Here's a freebie to get you started. I've created a list of 11 best topics that are appropriate for your first blog post to share with the world:

www.saravjeetsandhunetwork.com/11posts

Happy blogging!

Starting a Successful Blog

Share Your Passion and Turn It into a Business

Yes, that's right—start a successful blog to share your passion and turn it into a business, even if you don't have a single bone of entrepreneurship in your body!

If you want to start a blog and have no clue how to start and what to blog about, then you're in the right place!

You're going to learn exactly what you need to start your own WordPress blog.

* * *

Before I explain all the seven steps to start a blog, let's find out what a blog actually is and why you should blog.

What Is a Blog?

A blog, short for weblog, is a journal-style website consisting of articles and comments. Posts are typically displayed in reverse chronological order so the latest post appears at the top of the web page.

It's not to be confused with a website, as a blog is regularly updated.

Why Blog?

Blogging became popular after many entrepreneurs saw this as an important marketing tool.

A blog can be a home business in and of itself. Let's make it clear why you should have a blog.

- As a blog is updated continuously with new content, it's easy to keep your fans, customers, and clients up to date. Let them know about your deals and provide tips. The more prospects come to your blog, the more likely they're going to buy from you.

- Blogging is a great search engine optimization (SEO) tool because search engines love new content.

- Blogging can increase your audience very quickly. More valuable content means more readers who become your fans and customers. Your brand can grow tremendously.
- Prospects can subscribe to your blog right through the pop-up or other contact forms, so a blog can grow your email list tremendously.
- You can make money from your blog. Along with your own products, there are many ways to monetize it through affiliate marketing, advertising, etc.
- For lifestyle entrepreneurs, blogging can make a great option, as it is portable and flexible. The laptop lifestyle is becoming very popular these days.

So if you are looking to be an entrepreneur or home business owner, a blog can be a very convenient tool for your fast business growth.

Which Blogging Platform Should I Use?

WordPress is open source software that you can use to build beautiful websites and blogs.

I recommend wordpress.org, a free nonprofit platform where you have total control of your website. You can change anything, anytime you want. It's not to be confused with wordpress.com, a commercial platform designed to make money off your website. These two sites have totally different functions.

WordPress is a very simple program to build your website with different tools, plugins, widgets, themes, etc. Started in 2003, WordPress has evolved over time. Newbies can use it right out of the box with no tech knowledge at all. Tech-savvy people can customize it in many remarkable ways.

You barely have any control on your website or blog with wordpress.com just like Blogger, Weebly, Wix, etc. They want you to start with a free account, then they start charging you as you use their cart function to sell anything, but you barely have control of any other functions of your site, which is quite frustrating.

You want to own your website or blog. That's the correct way to build your business.

My first website was with Weebly. The swipe function was the only good part, but it was for a fee. You had no control over the rest, which was quite amateurish for a business website.

How I Got Started in Blogging

As soon as I finished my master's in literature, I became a high school teacher. I taught science, math, and English.

That ended abruptly as I got married and helped my husband in his brick-and-mortar business in New York. I had my children while working on and off in my neighborhood. I had always wanted to have a steady job, but I couldn't manage it because of my responsibilities as a mother and wife.

I worked a wide variety of jobs—a department store cashier, an admin assistant in health care agencies—but I didn't want to continue doing them for the rest of my life. I was fed up with the commute and the nine-to-five schedule of many jobs I had all these years.

I was always searching for ways to become my own boss. In September 2016, I started my blog. I love writing and teaching. Now I'm an online entrepreneur teaching people how to succeed online by starting their WordPress blog and empowering people to pursue their true passion through entrepreneurship.

I've been making videos since 2010. I started with YouTube. For over two years, I've been on Facebook Live videos for my blog.

How to Read This Book

Listed in this book are seven steps, and each has substeps. Go through each step consecutively without skipping. You'll have your blog up and running within a few weeks or so.

So let's dive into creating your WordPress blog.

Step 1: Domain Name

Find a domain name for your website. Brainstorm names for your blog. Find a friend or someone you trust and go through the names.

- Have an idea of what your domain name should be. Then go to GoDaddy or another host of your choice and see if that name is available.
- If it's available, that's good. If not, no worries. See what's available.
- Don't be afraid of long domain names.

I ended up getting saravjeetsandhunetwork.com after brainstorming with my neighbor-friend because saravjeetsandhu.com, the one I wanted, wasn't available. My full name happens to be long, but after adding the word network, it felt appropriate.

So take the time to choose the blog name you like. Otherwise, you have to live with it for the rest of your life.

Using your legal name for a domain name is often the best idea, but if you want to have a domain name after your hobby, passion, or your line of work, you can do that too.

There are simple options to get a clear domain name.

Suggestions when choosing a domain name

Go with the type of service. If you have a health and wellness blog, then the name can be something like healthyandfit.com.

Go with the audience. If you have a blog for new moms, the name can be mommyandbaby.com, or maybe lazybum.com for lazy people.

Go with the topic. If you are writing about traveling, the name can be easytravels.com, cheaptravels.com, etc.

If you're looking to make money right away with your blog, then do some keyword research (this term is defined and explained in Step 3) in your niche.

Find eight to ten top blogs in your niche. See what they're talking about, what they're writing about, and which of their posts are showing the most engagement.

Make a list of those keywords and figure out your blog name according to those so that when people are searching for some specific topic or thing, your blog will show up if you've done a good job in writing and SEO.

So now that you have figured out your domain name, purchase it and secure it at GoDaddy. GoDaddy, my domain name registrar, is very affordable and has good customer service.

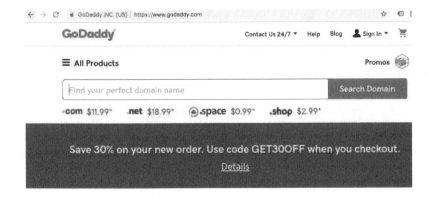

While registering, if you don't know or are unclear about something, always reach out for support either by chat or at the phone number provided at the website.

There are other few more other websites where you can purchase and register your domain/website/blog name such as namecheap.com and name.com.

Step 2: Hosting

Now that you have your website name registered with GoDaddy, the next step is hosting. Hosting is like having a house where you put things inside. Your website hosting is like a warehouse for your blog posts alongside many other functions such as audience, comment moderation, backup, etc. This is where they'll be hosted or stored.

Hosting is very affordable and doesn't cost you much at only $5 or less. You can choose any host you want.

Here's a list of the most popular hosting providers:

- Bluehost
- HostGator
- GoDaddy

Another good one is MyLeadSystemPRO. It's

convenient as it has everything in one package. I use it for hosting and my affiliate marketing plus many other features such as social media training, coaching, funnels, funnelizer, blog setup, customer relationship management (CRM), attraction marketing training, masterminding, and much more.

Check out the link below if you're looking for all the features to start your home business:

saravjeetsandhu.myleadsystempro.com

I recommend starting at a professional level so you can see all the benefits it provides, not just dipping your toes and not knowing other features.

Click on the Pricing tab. You'll find three plans.

In Basic plan, you don't have a blog.

In Professional plan, you have everything you need as an entrepreneur. If you pay an annual fee, you save 20 percent (you pay $125 per month instead of $149 per month), and you prevent the "quitting syndrome" when things get tough in online business as in any other business.

In Premium plan, you get everything plus personalized coaching and fast-track growth with personalized trainings.

Even if you want to be a member for one month, you have nothing to lose, as you're going to get current social media coaching and training courses by six-, seven-, or eight-figure earners such as Ray Higdon, Pat Flynn, and many other top industry leaders.

I started with MLSP in September 2016 with a risk-free trial ($10 for a 10-day trial) and never looked back!

Here is the link for the trial:

saravjeetsandhunetwork.com/special

Make sure your hosting company has a good reputation, excellent customer service, and good reviews from reputable sites.

Step 3: Setting Up WordPress

After registering your domain and buying your hosting service, you've laid out the framework for your blog. Now let's start designing it with WordPress!

First, install WordPress on your new domain with your web host's built-in tools. It's super simple. No HTML code or any other complicated technical things required.

WordPress software is already installed if you're with MLSP. When you're logged in to your MLSP member area, go to My Website tab, then click My Blogs/MLSP sites.

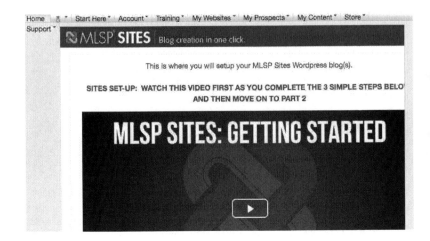

WordPress is going to ask you to set up your admin name for your site.

Pick an admin username and email so that you don't have to change once it's set up.

Save the information for later use so that you don't forget.

Once you log in, you're going to see your WordPress Dashboard.

Congratulations! You did it!

Your Dashboard is going to look something like this:

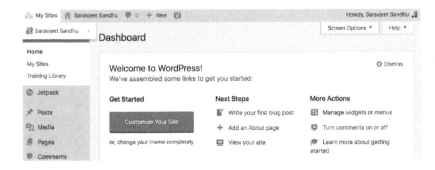

So now let's talk about plugins to customize your site with different features.

Plugins

- Choose and set up your basic WordPress plugins.
- Go to Dashboard and choose plugins. You're going to see a list of plugins available.
- For now, activate some important ones. We can activate the rest later as we need them.

Just like smartphone apps, plugins are apps for your website where you can customize and use your website for many different functions such as creating comments, blocking spam, putting opt-in forms, SEO, etc.

Do not select and activate all the plugins at the same time. That may slow down the functionality of your website.

Listed below are the important plugins you need to select and activate first.

Jetpack

Jetpack is a super powerful plugin. It's basically 20 plugins in one. Don't worry. You don't have to install all of them. You only activate the ones you need. You can always come back later to activate more.

To use Jetpack, a free plugin, you need to have your wordpress.com account. When you create your account, click the Select Free button or donate if you want to.

Go to your Dashboard and click Jetpack to activate it according to the directions that pop up. You'll need your API key from your wordpress.com account.

Yoast SEO

SEO is a strategy to drive more qualified traffic, leads, and sales to your website or blog. It affects the online visibility of a website or a web page in web search engines such as Google, Yahoo, and Bing. It's often referred to as organic results.

Yoast SEO is a WordPress plugin that guides you through many steps to optimizing your post.

It provides a checklist of things that you can correct step by step and also grades you on how well you've optimized your post.

- The images on this page are missing alt attributes.
- The SEO title is too short. Use the space to add keyword variations or create compelling call-to-action copy.
- This page has 0 nofollowed outbound link(s) and 2 normal outbound link(s).
- This page has 0 nofollowed internal link(s) and 1 normal internal link(s).
- The meta description contains the focus keyword.
- The length of the meta description is sufficient.
- The focus keyword appears only in 1 (out of 2) subheadings in your copy. Try to use it in at least one more subheading.
- You've never used this focus keyword before, very good.
- The focus keyword appears in the URL for this page.
- The text contains 462 words. This is more than or equal to the recommended minimum of 300 words.

You can read more about SEO on my blog post:

www.saravjeetsandhunetwork.com/whatisseo

This plugin is already installed and active if you're with MLSP. Otherwise, you have to install it.

Akismet

Akismet is a plugin that prevents spam comments on your blog.

To activate it, click Jetpack on the Dashboard on top and click Akismet Anti-Spam.

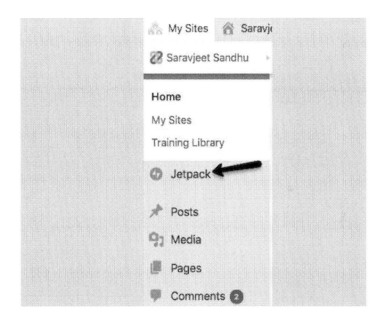

Set it up according to the video.

Akismet Anti-Spam (REQUIRED SETUP)

🗁 Plugins

Monarch

Monarch is a social media share button plugin for Facebook, Twitter, Google Plus, Pinterest, etc. Set this up if you want this on the side or any other spot.

Best Post For Facebook | Six Types of Posts For Social Media

Simple Social Icons

This plugin connects your viewers from your blog to other social media platforms. They don't have to look for them. They can see them on the blog. One click and they can also connect with you on other social media platforms right from your blog.

A Few More Awesome Plugins

Easy Facebook Like Box

This WordPress plugin allows you to display the customized Facebook feed on your website using the same color scheme of your website. It's completely customizable with lots of optional settings.

Better Click to Tweet

Add Click to Tweet boxes simply and elegantly to your posts or pages. It has all the features of a premium plugin for free.

'The most money is made outside your comfort zone"

> The most money is made outside your comfort zone.
>
> CLICK TO TWEET 🐦

Pinterest Widgets

Easily add a Pinterest follow button, pin widget, board widget, and profile widget to your site.

Contact Form 7

This is another WordPress plugin used to create sign-up forms.

* * *

There are many more plugins to use for different functions. You can discover and apply them gradually as needed as you go along and improve your writing skills.

Step 4: Themes and Domain Mapping

Themes

Go to your Dashboard. On the left-hand side of the menu, click *Appearance* and then *Themes*.

Choose a theme out of the many themes available. When I started, I chose the Simple theme by Genesis. Some themes are paid and some are free. Divi is the most popular paid theme.

Don't worry too much about the theme right now. It can also be changed later.

You can later hire someone as you make some more money to change your designs.

Get the one you can afford or a simple free one you like and start your blog without spending much time here because there are tons of themes. You can get lost in them for hours and days on end.

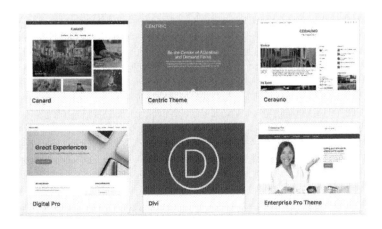

Domain Mapping

Domain mapping is another important way to customize your blog. Since you're using MLSP sites for your capture pages and campaigns, you need domain mapping. The step-by-step process is very easy. Simply follow the directions in the five-minute video.

You'll need your domain CNAME (canonical name record) in your registrar's (GoDaddy, Namecheap, etc.) account.

Go to your WordPress Dashboard, click Tools on the left-hand side of the menu, and then click Domain Mapping. Follow the directions in the video.

It's best to watch the training on one computer and keep pausing the video while applying the steps on another device such as your Mac or iPad.

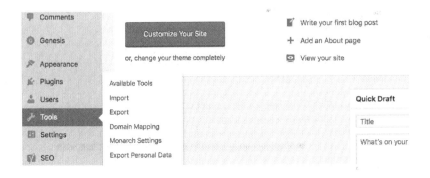

It can take up to 24 hours to show that your domain is mapped and valid.

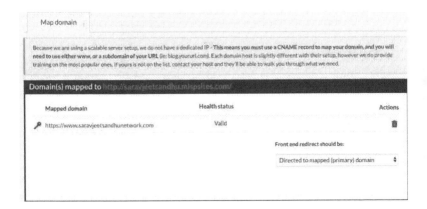

Step 5: Google Analytics and Webmaster Tools

Google Analytics

Make friends with Google so it can find your site and make you visible. Go to Google to search for Google Analytics or go to analytics.google.com. You'll need a Gmail account. If you do not have a Gmail account, get one now. Sign up for Google Analytics.

Fill in your info including your website info to get your tracking code. Just follow the easy directions to set up your account. Step-by-step instructions will show up, and you will get your tracking code.

Analytics

New Account

What would you like to track?

| Website | Mobile app |

Setting up your account

Account Name

Accounts can contain more than one tracking ID.

My New Account Name

Setting up your property

Website Name

My New Website

Website URL

http:// ▾   Example: http://www.mywebsite.com

Copy your tracking code and log into your WordPress Dashboard. Go to Settings on the left-hand side of the menu and select Google Analytics. Paste your Google Analytics tracking code in the field.

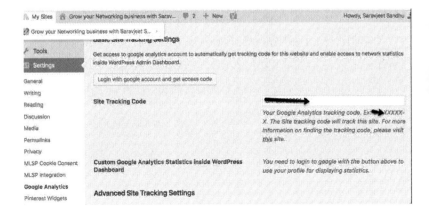

Give it a day or two. In 24-48 hours you can see the analytics of your website. You can even see in real time how many visitors are currently on your site. Isn't that cool?

Webmaster Tools

Next, add your new website to Google Webmaster Tools to maintain the health of your website so that Google can bring all the traffic to your website.

Go to google.com/webmaster/tools or search for Google Webmaster Tools on Google. You'll land on the same page.

Once you sign up, click *Add a Property* to add your website.

To verify your site, first click *Alternate methods* and select *HTML tag*, the easiest out of the methods shown on the image below:

There are a few methods shown over there, but select the HTML tag method, the simplest and easiest one.

You'll need a Google account to do this.

Once you get the code snippet, go to your WordPress Dashboard. Click SEO, then General, and then look for Webmaster Tools. Paste this code or meta tag in the Google field and click Save Changes. You're all set.

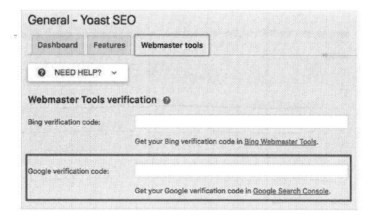

* * *

All right, this chapter seems a little complicated as you're starting out because this isn't something we see very often. I felt the same way too when I started out, but soon you'll get used to the terms as you hear and use them more often.

Give yourself a pat on the back that you have completed it!

The most important thing is writing good content. No content means no SEO. The easiest way to rank well for competitive search terms is simply to create high-quality content, but don't fuss too much over this, as Google's Search Engine Optimization (SEO) Starter Guide says, "Your ultimate consumers are your users, not search engines."

Focus more on providing good valuable content to your readers and consumers, and then work on SEO. Soon you'll get a grasp of it, so let's take a look at our next chapter!

Step 6: Setting Up Pages and Menu, Integrating with an Email Service Provider, and Freebies

Setting Up Pages

The best way to organize and design your WordPress site is to have different pages on the site aside from the blog page. People like to read blog posts for the info they're looking for, but after reading the info, they want to know who you are and how they can contact you, work with you, etc. by creating and organizing different pages such as *About Me* or *Work with Me*.

For now, create these pages, and later you can create other pages such as *Privacy Policy* and other pages you want to display.

To create a new page, go to your WordPress Dashboard, click *Pages*, and then click *Add*. Fill in the name of your new page, and below in the text section write what you want to display on your page.

Sara K. Sandhu

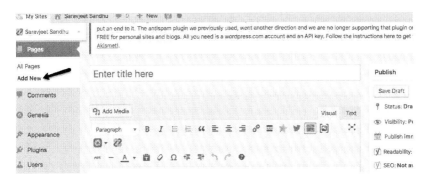

You can click *Preview* and see how your page will look once published.

You can publish it now or click *Save Draft.* That will save your draft for later review. You can publish it when you're ready.

Pages and posts have similar appearance and share same items, but they're different. Unlike pages, posts allow people to comment on them and interact with you. Pages are almost static or don't change often. They provide structure to your site. They affect the SEO of your site.

Sara K. Sandhu

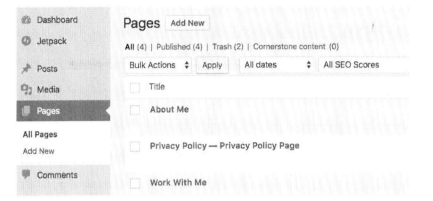

Menu

Menu is the primary way for people to navigate your site. It should be organized and thoughtfully put together. WordPress provides a simple Menu Editor for organizing and creating menus.

To create and manage menus, click the *Appearance* tab and *Menus* on your Dashboard, then type name in the Menu Name bar. Click *Save Menu.*

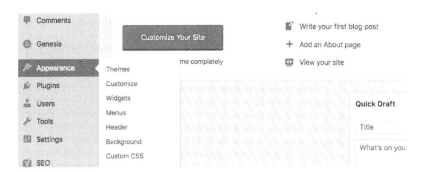

In the Pages box, you can choose a list of pages you've already created to put on your menu. Just check the Pages and click *Add to Menu.*

You can also add links from other sites by clicking on *Custom Links.*

Integrate with an Email Service Provider and Offer Freebies

Your purpose here is to connect with people who subscribe to your blog or people who opt in to your freebies and paid services so that you can follow up with them, send them info, stay connected to them in the future, and most importantly, build relationships with them so that they become your raving fans and customers.

You'll want to convert all your blog traffic into your leads and prospects so you can write for them and provide more value.

Check out this blog post I wrote. You'll have an excellent idea of what I'm talking about:

www.saravjeetsandhunetwork.com/
four-ways-to-convert-blog-traffic-into-leads/

You're going to need an autoresponder service for this.

If you haven't created your freebie or lead magnet, it's time to do so. It can be a checklist, cheat sheet, a video series, an e-book, etc.

When I had a small list, I used Mailchimp, a free service. I created a 10-step PDF and ran a contest to build my email list for free. And as your list grows, you pay a very small fee.

A free contest or a challenge is a very good and effective way to grow your email list without paying any single dime for advertising, but you have to have a freebie or lead magnet to do so. Your offer can be free coaching or a one-on-one session for half an hour, an hour, or however long you'd like.

Mailchimp is good for a small list of subscribers, but as you grow, you should look for email service providers with growth potential for your business.

Now I use AWeber email autoresponder service. I like it because it's easy to use with good customer support.

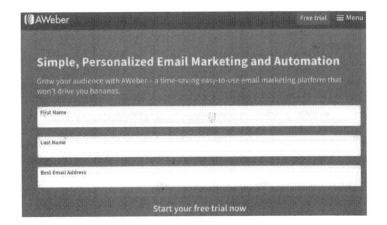

It has a 30-day free trial. Here is the link for you if you want to start:

http://aweber.com/?485364

There are many other email service providers such as GetResponse, ConvertKit, etc.

* * *

I've just given you an idea of these extra setups in steps 5 and 6 as they are necessary. You cannot skip them, but you can set them up later too as you write and go along. Otherwise, you can start writing your first blog post right after setting up WordPress in step 3. That said, here's a quote I like by Neil Patel: "Don't try to plan everything out to the very last detail. I'm a big believer in just getting it out there: create a minimal viable product or website, launch it, and get feedback."

Step 7: Writing and Monetizing Your Blog

Give yourself a big round of applause! Now you've set up your website to write your blog.

Now you can write about your passion and share it with the world while getting some raving fans and making money!

Click *Write your first blog post* or go to *Posts* on the left-hand side of the menu of your WordPress Dashboard. Click *Add new* and start writing your first post.

I wrote my story when I started posting. Start by either your story or any other topic you like or have researched.

There you go! Your first post is ready to present to the universe.

Congratulations! Let's celebrate!

A Simple Strategy to Write a Blog Post

Here's a tip on your first post: start by asking a question whose answer you know.

- **Creating Blog Post**
- **Introduce your Content: Ask a simple Question that YOU CAN answer**

That means you're knowledgeable enough to write about the subject. You can educate others about that through your writings, audios, videos, etc.

Congrats! You've just created your blog post!

Remember, your blog post must have a call to action (CTA), an instruction to the audience to provoke an immediate response. You tell readers what you want them to do. It doesn't always lead them to a sales page.

- **Creating a blog post**
- **Now it's time for the call to action (CTA)**
- **Simply tell them to get your updates, newsletter, marketing secrets etc.**

It can be a more detailed checklist of things to educate them more or a video you want them to watch so they'll go to the next step.

Examples: Sign Up, Register, Subscribe, Click Here for Free Download, Watch Now, Click Here, Buy Now, Learn More.

Your writing skills and blog will with improve with time, as everything takes time to grow.

Writing Strategy Planner

To write your content, you have to have a content strategy. Otherwise, you can keep blogging for years and will not see good results. When you have a strategy and map, then you know what direction you're going to and what you're writing. *You're going to monetize it* with your offers.

When you know ahead of time about what to write and when to write, you save a lot of your precious time and headache. Suppose you're writing for months, and now you don't want to write. After a month, you struggle to find a topic to write about, and you've already fallen off the wagon to write consistently. It's going to be much harder now to put up your blog, rank it, and see some good results.

I'm going to show you a good content strategy that works really well in my experience.

In your spreadsheet, choose a few categories you would like to blog about. Do not try to blog about everything under the sun and spread yourself too thin. Be an expert in a few things first and gain all the knowledge on them by reading books, articles, and blogs as well as watching videos and tutorials. Then blog about them. Later, as you become an expert, you can expand your categories or subjects.

BLOG CONTENT PLANNER						
Pub Date	Author	Post Type	Media	Category	Lead Magnet	Other
1/1/19	Your author name	How To Post	Video, Blog	Blogging Tips		3 Min Expert
2/1/19	Saravjeet	Day In the Life Post	Video, Blog	Social Media Tips	FB 3 Steps Marketing PDF	
4/1/19		List Post	Blog	MLM		
7/1/19						
10/1/19						
12/1/19						

Research your keywords and have a few planned headlines and topics that you're going to blog about in your niche. Try to match your freebies and offers with that topic so that you don't look salesy. Rather, you want to educate people about something while at the same time offering them something that has helped you that can also be beneficial to them.

Important Components of a Good Blog Post

Now I'll give you a few pointers for writing a good blog post that people will react to by liking and commenting on it. It makes them anticipate your next post.

There are many factors that go into making a good blog post, but I'm listing a few very important ones that can't be ignored at all.

If you want your post to rank higher in search engine results, you must use multiple strategies:

- Provide valuable content
- Perform keyword research
- Post videos
- Provide backlinks

Valuable Content

Everybody says, "Always post valuable content," but what is it, anyway? I'm going to break it down for you. When your post is providing a solution to some specific problem in your niche, then your post is a valuable post.

When someone is scrolling through the Facebook newsfeed and see the answer they are looking for, then your post is a valuable post. You are providing valuable content in the form of a solution to someone else's pressing problem.

When somebody has a challenge and your content is providing the answers, then your content is valuable content. So your valuable content is addressing some pains, some challenges, and some frustrations of your target market. That way, your prospects are going to like your post. They will be waiting for another solution on your next post.

You don't have to keep thinking about who's going to like your post when you publish it. The right people will be attracted to your valuable content. That's called attraction marketing.

If your valuable post is a Facebook Live video or a recorded one, then you can use this simple format:

- Question
- Content
- Call to action

Live video can be intimidating at first, but as you practice, it can bring faster results in your business. As the saying goes, the most money is made outside your comfort zone.

Keyword Research

People go to search engines such as Google and Yahoo or another platform such as YouTube to search for something.

Suppose someone is looking for a green smoothie recipe on Google and finds an excellent optimized blog post on a green smoothie that shows up in the search results on the first page. It means that the blog post is ranking higher than the other 50 or more blog posts on the same topic.

This same website also sells the ingredients of a green smoothie. Chances are, the reader buys all the ingredients listed there to make a smoothie after reading the post.

This is what everyone wants. People want their

blog posts to rank higher on Google and everyone looking for them should read them and buy from them.

So writing a post that will rank higher and bring you good revenue should be your goal.

If you first research relevant keywords in your niche to write a blog post, an article, or a book, it will have chances of ranking higher. There are tools for keyword research:

- Google Keyword Planner
- Keywords Everywhere
- SEO Book Keyword Tool
- and many others

Home › Extensions › Keywords Everywhere – Keyword Tool

 Keywords Everywhere - Keyword Tool `Add to Chrome`

Offered by: https://keywordseverywhere.com

★★★★★ 3,135 | Search Tools | ± 439,005 users

Overview   Reviews   Support   Related

I use Keywords Everywhere that you can download as a Google extension for Chrome or other browsers.

Google's Simple Search

Learning about keyword research is super important if you want to rank your post. That should be your goal when you write a blog post, but if you're a beginner, there is no need to confuse yourself much with all these tools.

As you become a seasoned writer, you're surely going to need all these tools to write an optimized post.

Other simple method to find your keywords for your blog post is to use Google on your browser. You can just google any topic to see what words and sentences Google comes up with. That can be very helpful in selecting your keywords for your topic.

Let's say you're looking for a home business. When you type *home business* in the Google search bar, all the sites listed on the first page have all the keywords in them, and the search terms listed at the bottom of the page have all the important keywords related to home business.

From here you're going to have a pretty good idea of keywords to use for your blog posts related to home business.

Searches related to homebusiness

successful home business

profitable home business ideas

home business ideas with low startup costs

home business opportunities

home business for moms

home business magazine

home based business ideas for moms

most successful home based businesses available today

1 2 3 4 5 6 7 8 9 10   Next

Video

Video is the fastest way to grow your audience and your brand. People can watch you, listen to you, and connect with you better on video.

Facebook Live

Facebook Live video is very popular and simple way to create videos. It can be very intimidating at first if you've never done a live video, but once you start and gradually progress, I promise you're going to create awesome videos.

I run Facebook Live video challenges in my group and teach people how to do Facebook Live videos and how to use them for business marketing. Here is the link to join BeYourOwnBoss, my Facebook group if you want to connect with other entrepreneurs and bloggers just like you: https://bit.ly/ownboss1

YouTube

You can record and upload your video to your YouTube channel and embed/share it on your blog. If you don't have a YouTube channel, you can start one. Go to youtube.com and set up your new channel to upload your videos. It is very easy to start your channel. You can even upload and save your Facebook Live videos to your channel.

Make sure you optimize your video for the YouTube requirement so that you can also rank on YouTube. Having a good title and description of your video makes your audience happy, as they know what your video is about. And you can share your video on other social media too such as Twitter, Pinterest, etc.

Backlinks

Backlink is a link one website gets from another website. Backlinks are considered very important in the ranking of a site in search engine results. The more links your website has, the higher you're going to rank.

The quality of links is very important. Links should be from authoritative websites. Links from authority sites rank higher than the links from nonauthority sites.

They should be natural and go with flow of the article, not stuffed in unnecessarily.

Here is my blog post explaining more about SEO and backlinks for beginners:

www.saravjeetsandhunetwork.com/whatisseo/

Monetizing Your Blog

It takes a lot of hard work, patience, and consistency to make money from your blog. If you're passionate about something, then you'll keep going even if you see no money for months. But if you started your blog only to make money, thinking this is the easiest part, you may or may not succeed. It takes money to make money. You have to spend money on training and courses so that you have all the knowledge to succeed.

When I started, I set up my blog in couple of weeks. It was up and running. I loved writing and teaching via video, but that doesn't mean I was getting enough traffic to my blog. I purchased a course on blogging and spent many weeks learning and applying all the techniques for a successful blog.

Check out the link to the course:

www.saravjeetsandhunetwork.com/3min

Here are a few important ways to monetize your blog:

- Sell your products: you can sell your own products that you've created such as cheat sheets, courses, e-books, etc.

- Sell affiliate products: you can sell the products of other people you have become affiliated with or those you use and recommend to your prospects.
- Advertising: You can use your blog for advertising products, either your own or affiliate products. The more exposure you get, the more sales you make.
- Provide a service or mentoring
- Consulting
- And so on

If you're a beginner, you obviously don't have a budget to spend on advertising, as you're trying to generate money for your business from your blog, so you don't have to spend a single dime at all.

The next thing to do is promote, promote, promote.

You can promote your blog posts on different social media, which is totally free. I promote on my Facebook Page for my business and in different Facebook groups in my niche.

When I upload my video on YouTube, I try to put excerpts from my blog post and sometimes the whole blog post in the description section. YouTube loves that. I send my new blog post to my email list immediately as soon as I publish it, and as soon as my post is published on my website, it gets automatically posted by IFTTT to my Facebook Page. IFTTT is a free platform to get apps and devices to work together when you set up the process.

I promote on Twitter by tweeting regularly about my blog posts. A few months back, I started using the very affordable SocialOomph for my automatic tweets.

I grew my audience on Twitter tremendously by sharing my blog regularly. I also do the same on other social media platforms such as Instagram, Facebook, Pinterest, and YouTube.

The more exposure to your blog post gets, the more people are going to show up and engage with your post, and the more prospects are looking for what you have to offer.

Plenty of leads can lead to plenty of sales, not the other way around.

You won't improve your writing skills and make

money from your blog overnight, but if you apply what I teach here, be persistent, and keep honing your skills, soon you're going to have a large following and revenue. As Eric Worre of Network Marketing Pro says, "My world changed when I started focusing on the skills and made the commitment to practice, practice, practice until I mastered them."

Now you know how to write an optimized, valuable blog post, and you have your writing strategy and planner, freebies, and offers.

So now blog your heart out and share on all social media platforms to grow your brand and make money.

Congratulations!

You've finished the book, so go write and promote!

* * *

Reviews

If you've liked this book, please leave me a review on Amazon. It takes a couple of minutes, but it helps me tremendously and keeps me busy writing.

For support and posting your first blog, join my Facebook group, BeYourOwnBoss:

https://bit.ly/ownboss1

Free PDF download:
www.saravjeetsandhunetwork.com/11Posts

Wishing you all the very best always!

Sara K. Sandhu

* * *

Made in the USA
Columbia, SC
23 July 2020